10/27/89

Junie & to
God ble..
children and they are the
joy of our life. I'm proud
to have you as mine, we are
proud of you both. It is
never to late to pursue
your dreams, and they
can come true. I love
you all and pray for each
of you daily! Keep
reaching for that goal and
you'll reach that far off
"Star". God bless you,
Love,
Mom

The Winning Formula

The Winning Formula

Prayer + Faith + Physician = Healing

Dr. Gloria J. Keene, Ph.D.

VANTAGE PRESS
New York

The opinions expressed herein are solely those of the author. Each individual should seek the advice of his or her own physician before starting any new medical program.

Cover design by Polly McQuillen

FIRST EDITION

Published by Vantage Press, Inc.
419 Park Ave. South, New York, NY 10016

Manufactured in the United States of America
ISBN: 978-0-533-15554-5

Library of Congress Catalog Card No.: 2006905097

0 9 8 7 6 5 4 3 2 1

To those I am most grateful to . . .

Beloved, I pray that you may prosper in all things and be in health, just as your soul prospers.

—John 3:2

Contents

Acknowledgments

My parents, Javie W. and Mary M. McIntyre, provided me a Christian foundation that has been a source of guidance, support, and comfort to me. They were examples that I used to set and chart my course in life, for which I am eternally grateful. They were instrumental in the paths I chose to pursue. My father died of an asthma attack, at the age of 48 (I was 16 at the time), but I had already learned valued life lessons from him, such as faith in God is of utmost importance, we are to live as responsible beings, and we should value each day that we have.

My mother influenced and encouraged me as a child and into my adult life. It was during her last years of life that I saw the depth of her magnitude of her own faith and trust in God. She spent her last 4–5 years in a hospital bed in her home. She never allowed herself to become depressed or succumb to self-pity. Instead, she encouraged and lifted the spirits of those who came by to do just that for her. She got through those painful bedridden years by her faith and love for God. She taught me that it is not all about ourselves, but about being a witness for God and an example to others of what He can do.

Mrs. Hyacinth Tennessee, my fifth grade teacher, made me feel as if I could do just about anything. She always found time to talk to me and encourage me, and often gave me an opportunity to show what I could do. But it was as an adult that I learned even more about her as a person.

She had a tremendous faith in God and was also an example of how to endure serious illness while being confronted by death itself. Even though she was terminally ill, she continued to attend Bible study classes to learn more about the God she loved so much. She said, "I am getting closer to Him all the time!" I shared with her that when I was a child she made me feel I could do anything. She said to me, "I could see even then that you could!"

Last, but certainly not least, I want to acknowledge my husband, Bill Keene, Sr.; he has encouraged me during our marriage in all things I've set out to do. He has been nurturing and has enabled me to meet and conquer many challenges. My children have also encouraged my efforts and always said (yelled), Go for it! They made me feel very loved and appreciated. Above all, I thank God for keeping and carrying me at all times.

Introduction

There have been gradual strides in the past in the area of medicine in regards to the acceptance of God and faith in patient care. Acknowledging the need for Christian faith in God to be included has been slowly finding acceptance by medical professionals. But more recently it has stepped up in pace, and the reality of this has become clearer. In the past, medical professionals preferred the separation of medicine and Christian spirituality.

Many doctors were afraid to address their patients in regards to their faith because they thought it to be inappropriate, they were not professionally adequate themselves to address it, or out of fear of some negative consequences. They merely asked the patient's religious preference or denomination, or if they practiced any faith or belief. Some physicians are Christians themselves, yet still avoid such matters when treating their patients. Other physicians fall into the category of atheist or not actively practicing their religious belief.

In the past two or three years, there have been numerous television programs, special reports, and newspaper and magazine articles that addressed faith involvement in medicine. Today it is becoming more obvious to people that consideration needs to be given to the benefits of faith being included in the health care treatment. Medical schools are adding courses of study on faith and belief to the curriculum for the students. Resources, reference materials, and books are now available on the benefit of including faith in the medical care for patients.

Faulty appliances must be returned to the manufacturer if they are to be covered under warranty. The mindset is that the company is the expert since they created or made the product. God created all things; He formed the heavens and all in the universe. God designed and created man in His own image, down to every minute detail. He alone had the power, knowledge, and capabilities to do such an awesome thing. He gave the doctors their knowledge and skills to treat the ills of mankind. God is the expert in repairing and restoring us to health or miraculously curing us, and He should be more than welcomed in the treatment process.

Physicians could practice medicine or study forever and could not exceed or even match God's ability in healing in any way! Only God can cure a terminally ill patient, or cause a hole in a heart to close without surgery, or reverse conditions considered to be irreversible (i.e., cell or organ degeneration, emphysema, or AIDS). But just imagine what a doctor could do when he includes faith and spirituality (bringing God in the midst of it all) as part of the medical treatment program. The comfort and assurance that Christ can bring is not even measurable in terms of benefit to the patient and his or her family.

Illness is something that we all prefer not to deal with, therefore, we want support from others at those times. A team approach is the best way to address healing and recovery for a patient. Patients need a support team and the team concept would allow the addressing of all their concerns, including stress, fear and anxiety. They need faith, prayer, and the reassurance of hope rather than sentiments of concern or empathy alone from others.

The doctor's primary concern is to treat the physical

symptoms and rectify body malfunctioning due to disease or illness so as to eliminate the patient's suffering. The physician tries his best to reassure the patient by saying that he's treated this condition hundreds of times, the procedure to be performed is quite simple, this treatment is the latest method available, and recovery success rates are high. That is about all the doctor can give a patient to address the fears or concerns of the patient. They have little or no time to counsel the patient otherwise.

Without faith and prayer being a part of medical treatment, stress and anxiety over the condition just add to their symptoms and could prolong recovery time. Stress and worry can elevate blood pressure, make the pain more intense, and affect other things as well, such as immune system resistance levels and potential for infections. Stress can rob the patient of their proper sleep and rest, which are needed for recovery. Lengthy recovery time results in longer periods out of work, which can add yet another stressor, the stress of financial burden or hardship.

Medicine is not an exact science; therefore, the patient needs every advantage possible. The best advantage is God and He should not be considered optional, He should be right in the middle of it all! There are illnesses that require more than traditional support and treatment, so more support and more encouragement is the only way to go. When there is great uncertainty as to what to do, why not go to the only certain source available, our creator, God, our Father.

Traditionally, change is rarely readily accepted by everyone. Some people resist change of any kind, no matter how minimal. An example of this in the medical field would be the role of nurse practitioner, which was added to the medical staff not so many years ago. Many patients were not thrilled with the idea of this person examining, diagnosing, and prescribing medication for them. They could not get past the title "nurse practitioner." Some patients felt they were medically at risk if they were seen or treated by this new professional. Others grumbled about being charged the same amount for the visit as if they had seen the doctor. But the nurse practitioner is exceptionally well-trained and is qualified to do these duties.

On the *700 Club* on television, a doctor that had treated Ron Winan, brother of BeBe and CeCe Winan, internationally known gospel singers, for a serious heart condition talked about the miracle of prayer. The doctor considered Ron Winan's case to be terminal and impossible for him to survive. The doctor called the family together to give them the news and to allow them to see him for a final time.

The physician was not familiar with this family of strong faith. He was unaware that the father and several of the brothers were ministers and that the whole family had great faith. They all circled around Ron's bed and held hands as they called out on the name of Jesus and interceded with God on their brother's behalf. Because they would not accept defeat by the enemy and because they knew that they needed to bring in the true and best physician that ever existed, which is God, they prayed sorely to heaven.

Once they added their faith, their brother received a miraculous recovery from what was considered terminal and impossible. The surgeon was amazed at what he witnessed and on national television, he vowed to pray with each of his patients from that day on!

God has always shown His power and that He is ultimately in control, because He loves us and His desires our trust in Him. We need to incorporate counseling, prayer, and faith in God in all areas of our lives, especially in medicine. The benefits of this are too numerous to list, and it needs to begin right now. When physical or mental health issues are addressed, our faith and spirituality must be a part of the healing process.

The Winning Formula

One

What Causes Sickness?

Today society has an epidemic of crises, stress, and problematic conditions. Like never before, we work and live in environments that breed stress and crisis situations non-stop. Millions of people exist daily in extremely trying and stressful situations, and they view it as a way of life. Many feel it will go away, some feel that they cannot take it much longer, and some are not as affected as others by life's pressures. The difference is basically how they each view their situation, and ultimately how they handle it. Their response to things in their life is the key to how they survive the hurdles of life.

Many people are so devastated that they allow a crisis to ruin their careers, marriages, and even their health. Crisis is capable of causing panic or anxiety attacks, desperate actions, or even uncalculated decisions, with even more negative consequences. Stress can sometimes be prevented or minimized, but even when we plan well and move with caution, we may not be able to avoid a situation from happening. I have often thought that those who give little or no thought to their plans or actions use tons of thought trying to clean up a mess that they have created.

Health experts say that we have too many people succumbing to serious illnesses that could have been prevented. We want fast, easy eating, and it would appear that

1

we don't even have the time to set up a pressure cooker to use. We want to "nuke" every time we prepare a meal. There are many serious problems that are the direct result of using the "trusty" microwave oven. To name a few, burning yourself during removal of hot foods or liquids, or while trying to eat food right out of the microwave when it's steaming hot; ingesting chemical residue from using plastic containers in the microwave; over-cooking and destroying nutrients; or over-drying or making meats tough, which causes indigestion.

We feel we are too busy to prepare food at home, so we resort to take out meals, delivery pizza, fast food burgers, specialty fried chicken, and sodium-loaded frozen entrees, all of which have at least two billion calories and millions of milligrams of sodium. Our health is a large part of the wholeness we are trying to achieve and maintain. Health experts say that we are actually shortening our own lives, and creating a sickly next generation of our children.

God gave Adam and Eve a garden with fruits and vegetables, because healthy eating was his plan for our lives. Some people feel that Adam and Eve had no choice, and they would have pigged out on fast food, too, had it been available to them. But if you think about it, Eve had only one curiosity and that was to see what was so special about the apple they were forbidden to eat, and to see if they would surely die. Satan had his fingerprints all over the scene of this crime. He said, "Try what you have been deprived of and surely you will not die." He said, "God does not want you to have knowledge." What a liar!!

Man started to mess up at that point and hasn't stopped since. God did not create anything detrimental to our health, but we did. Man created and invented all of the things that are harmful to us physically, mentally, emotionally, and spiritually. God is not a God who would create us in His image and then create all means and methods of harmful things to endanger us. We alone take credit for those things that are detrimental to us. Some people pursue wealth and prosperity at the risk of destroying or wiping out everything in existence, if necessary. We all need to be in fervent prayer on the behalf of the greedy people who pursue wealth at any cost.

Repeated disobedience, ignorance of the word, or too little time in the word leaves us open to whatever happens at the hand of the enemy. The enemy comes to rob, kill, and to destroy you. He has no good will for you, at any time; therefore, do not be deceived by his cunning tactics. He wants to prevent us from fulfilling or achieving our divine destiny and walking in sound health. It is when we let our guard down that he can weaken us spiritually and attack our physical body and health. He has a mean right hook; if we are lax in the reading of the word, our strength and power is at a low level. But having a good supply of the word within us and faith even as small as a mustard seed, we can knock his "lying and smelly" (odor of evil) socks off!

In addition to our eating habits, which leave a lot to be desired, we follow the poor diet up with even poorer exercise habits. We are of the push-button flick-the-remote generation, or the couch potato mentality. We make the couch potato seem like the "fitness guru," because it is so popular, even with our kids.

Too often we fail to see the expense, financial and physical of the easy way out. We readily pay exorbitant prices for the wonderful riding lawn mower (even for tiny lawns), and many people knowingly and unlawfully park in handicapped areas to save a few steps. The uncanny part is that they pray that they don't get a parking ticket or get towed. We all like to try the latest in technology if it will require us to use less of our own processing thoughts. It is a sad day when we are too lazy to process thoughts or use our God-given intelligence. It is said that Einstein was a great genius, but many don't know that he only used approximately 10% of his brain power or knowledge. It is also thought that keeping the brain active can prevent dementia. So we could be encouraging the onset of our developing dementia in our future.

Most homes today have all kinds of save-a-step products, tools to reach with, easy-does-it equipment, "no brainer" type instructions on "how to," and you name it. Quick and easy the goal, and life the simpler are the rules. We fail to remember that the healthiest people were people that farmed, did their work by hand, plowed, and prepared foods without fancy gadgets or mixes.

Poor diet, lack of exercise, and too much stress can cause us to possibly have hypertension, diabetes, cancer, heart disease, or stroke. We have a choice; in fact, the quality of our choices will determine the quality of our lives and health. Ask yourself a question, "Who am I hurting and am I being selfish in regards to making choices?" I think you already know the answer. Are you pleasing God when you treat your body and mind this way? Be honest. Of course you are not pleasing God.

Being healthy and physically fit does not prevent stress or crisis, but you are able to deal with them better emotionally and with less physical repercussions if you are fit. You will have more emotional control and your thought processes will be more alert and effective. Our responses and reactions have the power to make things better or worse in a situation. Once we take action, it is not always possible to undo that action. Prayer and thought can avoid ruin or embarrassment, and it can preserve our health.

People used to ask a person who was obviously upset,

"What's eating you?" Actually, stress does devour our health if we allow it to do so. It affects our nerves, heart, digestive system, blood pressure, and other things as well. Unless stress is managed, it will bring illnesses, which can decrease our enjoyment of our lives, or it can even cause premature death.

A person can decrease their stress by using antidotes to it, such as exercise, relaxation, and visualization techniques, or cut off the source of stress. These ways of managing stress are very effective and safe as well. I would not recommend that people take drugs to address or deal with stress in their lives. Some people go to their doctor seeking medication for stress and their nerves. They may be prescribed Xanax or Valium for nerves, and get something like Ambien to help them sleep at night. These are like putting a band-aid on cancer. It won't stop the cancer from spreading, nor will it cure the cancer. These medications for nerves and sleeplessness will always be needed because the problem isn't being dealt with, merely covered up. They are also addictive, thus another potential problem.

There are others who do not go to seek medication to help them cope with stress because they rely on other sources that are readily accessible to them. Some of them will smoke heavily, resort to drinking alcohol, over-medicate themselves on pain pills or resort to overeating. Use of these alternative methods are still unhealthy, and some of these can be addictive as well.

People fail to realize or take seriously that they can cause some chronic illnesses by drinking, smoking, and overeating. They can also affect the lives of others with their behaviors, through secondhand smoke, or driving under the influence of alcohol for instance.

Smoking itself can bring on a multitude of problems, such as stroke, hypertension, asthma, emphysema, mouth, throat, or tongue cancer, chronic bronchitis, heart disease, and lung cancer. We can't leave out the potential of accidental fires from unsafely handling cigarettes, lighters or matches.

Harmful Emotions

Anger is a very destructive emotion, with many negative results. Because anger is such a negative force, we should not hold it inside; it will manifest itself internally as some form of illness. Letting go of anger does not mean that we let go of it in an explosive manner. We should learn to manage our stress, anger, or anxieties, and counseling is available for those who cannot control their actions when angry.

We all get angry at times, but the result of that anger depends on how we manage that emotion at the time. I remind myself that Jesus got angry, but he did not sin. He is our best example of how we are to act or be in life, in all situations. People that have a real problem with anger management need to seek professional help, or eventually reap serious consequences.

Ron and Pat Potter-Efron, in their book *Letting Go of Anger*, list what they consider the ten most common anger styles. The styles they listed are as follows:

1. **Anger Avoidance:** Anger avoiders don't like anger much; some are afraid of their anger or the anger of others. They gain the sense of being a good or nice person because they don't get mad. They often don't get angry even when something is wrong, so anger doesn't help them survive.

2. **Sneaky Anger:** Anger sneaks never let people know they are angry. In fact, they don't know how angry they are.

When others get mad at them, anger sneaks can look hurt and innocent. Anger sneaks gain a sense of control over their lives when they frustrate others.

3. **Paranoid Anger:** This occurs when someone feels irrationally threatened by others. Those with paranoia see aggression everywhere. They trust nobody, and worse, they have poor judgment because they confuse their own feelings with those of others.

4. **Sudden Anger:** People with sudden anger gain a surge of power. They release all their feelings, to feel good or relieved. Loss of control is a major problem with sudden anger and they can be violent.

5. **Shame-Based Anger:** People who need a lot of attention or are very sensitive to criticism often develop this anger style. The slightest criticism sets off their own feeling of shame. They don't like themselves and feel worthless, not good enough, or unlovable.

6. **Deliberate Anger:** Deliberate anger is planned. People who use anger this way usually know what they are doing. They like to control others and are sometimes violent.

7. **Addictive Anger:** They want or need the strong feelings that come with anger; their adrenaline rushes. Anger isn't fun, but they look forward to the emotional "high."

8. **Habitual Anger:** Habitually angry people get angry about small things. They gain predictability. Their main feeling is anger and anger runs their lives.

9. **Moral Anger:** These people feel they have a right to be angry when others have broken a rule. Morally angry people gain the sense that their anger is for a good cause.

10. **Hate:** Hate is hardened anger. It happens when someone decides that at least one person is totally evil or bad.

I am sure that we all realize that it is natural to get angry at some time or another, and it is normal to do so. It is not good to allow that anger to hurt you or someone else. Anger needs to be addressed and then let go. Addressing anger does not mean that you become violent, destructive, or even bitter. We must deal with our anger in the appropriate manner, taking control of it and not letting it control our actions.

When a person allows their anger to get out of control on a regular basis, it is time to seek anger management from a counselor. Ephesians 5:26–27 tells us, "Be angry, and do not sin . . . do not let the sun go down on your wrath, nor give place to the devil." Giving place to the devil means allowing him to use you in or because of your anger. So the scripture states that we can be angry, but the problem comes in when we allow that anger to encourage or cause us to sin.

Anger turned inward or avoided causes illnesses in our bodies such as ulcers, nervousness, headaches, allergic reactions, heart problems, and lots of other psychological sicknesses.

Patients that are ill need to know that their illnesses may be a result of their attitudes about life, decisions they have made, fears, overworking, and even anger they have. Teaching them to forgive, relax, not worry, and include prayer and faith in their lives is just as important as the physician's treatment and medicine prescribed. These things need to be part of their overall care.

God's plan for our lives is very simple. We must live by God's word and the example of Jesus. If we live by the Bible and learn its teachings, we would not go through a lot of the unnecessary or undue hardships we experience. The times may change, but God's word and promises will always be the same. The Bible addresses every situation and circumstance possible in life.

The major expressions of anger are bitterness, resentment, and bad attitudes. Kenneth Stafford, author of *Handbook for Helping Others,* states that "bitterness is detected first in a person's speech and then his attitude. Bitterness leaves a trail of broken relationships and obscures one's vision of life. It severs one's relationship with God. As a result, we become insensitive to God's word and violate it."

Resentment is a negative, hostile feeling, caused by not getting what we want, when we want it. Those of resentment do not wait for the blessings of God and His timing. They are of the now mindset. "The mind set on flesh is hostile toward God; for it does not subject itself to the law of God, for it is not even able to do so; and those who are in the flesh cannot please God" (Romans 8:7–8).

Unforgivingness is also an expression of anger. We must make the decision to forgive those who have willfully wronged us, or it will remain a part of us until we do let it go. We are telling the devil to get lost when we don't accept his antics about our having the right to be angry and we should resent the people that hurt or wronged us. He will quickly get to stepping when we turn over our unforgiving spirit to God for cleansing. We need to accept the fact that it is a sin to not forgive.

Author Kenneth Stafford says, "Depression usually occurs when emotions are not healed. It is caused by a sinking of the spirit, evident in a feeling of guilt, hopelessness, or unworthiness. Failure to control or discipline yourself generally leads to depression. It occurs when a person gives in to negative emotions, rather than responding to a problem God's way, which will lead to a positive solution."

Negative emotions that lead to depression are fear, anger, and guilt. If you know someone that has depression, they may have fears, be angry about something, or be experiencing some guilt about something they may have done. They may also fluctuate between those emotions or display them together. Whatever the source of those emotions, the person may need some counseling and prayer to seek healing for wholeness. Depression is a serious matter and it should be treated as such. It can cause a person to live a life of hell, or it can cause the person to commit suicide. God intended neither of those things for a person's life. The negative emotions of fear, anger and guilt can be a result of unresolved root problems such as unforgiveness, negligence, self-pity, stress, rejection, financial need, sexual problems, lingering illness, lack of daily schedule, resentment, family conflicts, bad relationships, failure, loneliness, lack of self-discipline, loss of a loved one, fatigue, or poor self-image. A person can be so depressed that they have no motivation to do anything, at any time. They just exist and barely do that.

Psychosomatic illnesses that are brought on or encouraged by stress or negative emotions we succumb to can lead to organic dysfunction. Our emotions negatively affect our physical health or wellness. Some possible psychosomatic illnesses are hypertension, headaches, colitis, kidney stones, heart conditions, arthritis, low back pain, or gallstones. We don't set out to create lifestyle habits, behaviors, or activities that lead to sin, sickness, and disease, but it happens. Some do it out of ignorance, anger, or even revenge. Whatever the reason, once we realize that we are out of God's will, out of fellowship with Him, we need to cut off that sin! The sooner, the better because the longer we linger in ways that are against God, the more the illness progresses.

Where do we go from here and how do we get a grip on what to do next? I say that we need to go back to the very beginning. In the beginning was God's word and it still is what we are to listen to, follow, keep, and live by. It surely makes sense to me. God has guidelines and instruction for everything in life. Our health is important, and without it we can not serve Him effectively, nor can we be a testimony of His faithfulness.

We are to put God in the middle of our health issues and the treatment process because ultimately He is the healer. I call Him my Chief Physician, Head Surgeon, and my Miracle Provider, all rolled into one. I know that only God can truly mend or restore my broken body, mind, or spirit. With the Lord on our side and in the middle of our care at the time of our illness, we have hope, comfort, and support like no other. The medical staff needs all the extra help and assurance they can get as well. When God is in the midst of it all, everyone involved gets the support that's needed.

By Jesus' stripes we are healed because He died for our sins, which means our sins are forgiven us. That tells me that He bled and died on the cross for me, and that also tells me that my healing meant a W-H-O-L-E lot to Him. He is entitled to and deserves first place in my sick room, right in the middle of it all. We should forget not His good and tender mercies, nor His wonderful benefits. I have truly tasted and the Lord is G-O-O-D!

God is the master designer of our complete being and we cannot say that the doctors don't need Him to direct their treatment of our illness. When doctors include faith and prayer in treatment of patients, it lifts some of the weight off their shoulders. They have less of a sense of pressure due to the fact they are not in this alone and their faith combined with the faith of the patient is what God wants. It is asking Him to move on their behalf. It is saying if a miracle is to happen, it will come through the Lord.

God honors the prayers of those with a sincere heart and belief in Him. When we give God recognition, praise, and worship Him in truth, nothing stands in the way of His blessing us. He will bless the patient and the physician. When a doctor admits his weaknesses and says he needs God in treating the patient and gives God the glory for restoring health to the patient, the benefits are many. Bringing God into our illness and healing sets the stage for a miracle. We should praise Him continually!

Two

Counseling As a Part of Healing Sickness

Preparing the mind to deal with health problems is very essential. The ability to mentally process what is happening in our body, understand the condition, and grasp what is necessary for healing requires that the patient is not stressed. We need to be able to focus calmly on following the treatment plan prescribed by the doctor. Our mind, body, and spirit need to be in one accord at the time of the healing process.

Preparing a person for surgery, therapy, or ongoing treatment of any kind requires that they be able to pull on any strengths or resources available to them. The mind and emotions are two components in healing the whole person. Romans 12:2 says, "You will be transformed by the renewing of your mind." Counseling can be used to help a person prepare emotionally and spiritually for surgery, as well as used during the healing process.

In regards to surgery for a patient, the patient would benefit from pre- and post-surgery counseling. Pre-surgical counseling would benefit the patients by helping them to be calm and accepting of the need for the surgery, and remain in an optimistic frame of mind. It could encourage them in the use of their faith and prayer. It would allow them the opportunity to voice any concerns or issues they need to address before the procedure is performed. This is what the physician does not have ample time to do or give them.

Counseling a patient prior to surgical procedures can help lessen or reduce worry, tension, and stress over the seriousness of the operation. Thus, pre-operative anxiety and post-operative depression may be avoided, or at least minimized. Counseling can encourage patients of all medical concerns to use faith and prayer to resist the fear that Satan tries to inflict on them. It reinforces the positives of the great love Christ has for them and the fact that He is with them in all things.

The patient needs to know that they must call upon their personal faith as a resource; they must gain knowledge of what their responsibilities are in their care and recuperation. They need to be responsible and obedient in following the prescribed medical treatment and trusting God for healing. Patients need to be reminded that praising God, especially during illness, has a healing effect on them. They usually are so absorbed in their feelings at the time that they are not thinking in the right or their usual mindset.

A counselor can help them to focus and use some relaxation techniques, which in turn will allow them to place their mind on the Lord and to gain emotional strength as support to them. Thinking of God can help them to experience a calm and quiet so they can rest. Their pain is lessened because the tension that increases the intensity of the pain has been reduced, which in turn may lower blood pressure (the old cause and effect principle).

The spiritual inclusion in the healing process is of the utmost importance. We need to acknowledge God, and give Him the credit and glory for healing. We cannot make any progress in the area of healing without Christ Jesus. We cannot treat a person completely and restore them to wholeness unless we address all three components, mind, body, and spirit. God created us with all three, so to leave out one of them is not holistically wise. The need for each of them is indicated because God deemed them necessary, or He would not have included all three. God created us in His image; we cannot neglect any aspect of our being.

Sickness requires our attention and our efforts to heal. We can do a better job of restoring our health if we are calm and able to center our focus. We need to use prayer and communication with God to bring the relaxation we need to reduce stress and its effect on our body. God is our peace and our strong tower in all situations in life.

Have you ever wondered why the majority of people today seek "quickie" fixes for everything in our lives. It's mostly because we have become accustomed to the instant, speedy mentality afforded us through computerized and the new age automation system. But God's word says that patience is a virtue. God himself took six days to create the universe and heavens, and rested on the seventh day. How is it that we feel that we must have it all and have it right now! Many people get annoyed when they are kept waiting or told that there will be a lengthy time involvement.

For us to give birth to another life, we must carry the baby for nine months for the baby to be fully developed and not at health risk. God desires that things be done in order, done well, and without rushing. Healing is a process and we must learn to do it in order, putting God and faith first. Christians are not to refer to themselves as merely religious folk. Anything can be done religiously, which indicates or refers to something done rigidly or habitually, and without changing. Christians are people of faith and belief in God, following in the steps of Christ Jesus.

God's word indicates that we are to use wisdom and that we are to seek counsel in matters when we need it.

In the scriptures there were many people who counseled: scholars, scribes, priests, prophets, ministers, deacons, physicians, and many people who were called on to help those in areas on which they needed counsel. We will have times in our lives that we feel that we can't cope with what is happening in our lives. Counseling is for those times and it is a source of support. There should be no stigma attached to getting counseling.

Stigmas about getting counseling are straight from the devil; he doesn't want you to get help because he wants you to be weak, afraid, and vulnerable. Let's face it, he wants you to fall. He is also behind the thoughts of the doctor who feels you should not have faith and prayer in the middle of your treatment. Nine times out of ten, that doctor is not in a relationship with the Lord, or does not believe in the Lord, or is of the mindset he is "all that" and he is all you need to get well. Narrow minds are a source of limited knowledge and we as Christians know that is not what God intends for us.

Luke was Paul's physician and he attended to his medical needs. We know from scripture that God had people of all gifts, talents, and knowledge to address the many needs that we would be faced with in life. God has a grand scale plan for our lives, and He has put all the pieces in place for us to live an abundant life. In fact, God sent Jesus to assure us of that abundant life. You see, God has a plan for our success.

Life without the inclusion of the Lord is a sad life indeed. I would not do anything that I could not include God in and have Him in charge of. Life without faith, worship, praise, and reverence of the Lord is a life that will be full of woes. But placing all four of those acts in the midst of treatment for healing is the primary component for restored health. The first thing you need to have in this formula would be your prayers, then add faith, the doctor, and medicine.

The counselor is an asset to the physician because they will address the patient's anxieties, concerns, and add support, which affords the doctor the opportunity to address the medical issues only. When the doctors think about it, they rely on the nurses, laboratory technicians, radiologists, and other people to be a part of the treatment team. I know that they are all in the medical field, but it still says that he needs to call in others to treat the patient successfully. But when you think about the fact that counseling helps to address the matters that may be influencing the health problems of the patient, it is logical to include a counselor.

Bringing God in the middle of the treatment team is likened to bringing in "the" specialist, not to consult, but take charge and be the "expert." Christian counseling has been deemed at times by secular counselors as, "Okay, in its place." But I like to see them explain to God how He, our creator, with His infinite wisdom, does not have a place in treating a person medically or psychologically. I tell you what, I would not want to be standing within 100 feet of them when they do it!

Using wisdom in all things is what God expects of us. We would never (in our right mind), think of asking our hair stylist for medical advice and we would definitely not ask our auto mechanic for advice on hair problems. I don't know about you, but I would immediately get off an airplane in which the co-pilot announced that the pilot did not show up and he himself wasn't feeling well, proceeding to ask for a volunteer to help him out up front of the plane, just in case.

The above scenario may be an extreme example of having to use sound wisdom or judgment, but you may be surprised that some people would have trouble deciding whether or not to get off the plane. The co-pilot has to have enough skills and knowledge to fly the plane on his own. But in the event that he is not feeling well could be a potential heart attack or stroke, or even death, that volunteer to assist him would not know beans about navigation of the plane or safe landing. Of course, there would never be a decision like that to make because the airline's policy and procedures would not allow it.

Dr. Dale A. Matthews, M.D., author of *The Faith Factor*, states that, "Our prayer life with God and our belief in Him enables us to have a stronger psychological well-being and less distress. Being involved in church activity, surrounded by other believers and a sense of support for each other, affords you a deeper level of psychological health." I am delighted to find that some doctors are realizing the value and necessity of prayer, faith, and support for our well-being. Addressing health issues to heal the person requires that we include the spiritual and psychological as well to achieve the well-being of the individual.

Life has many things that we must resolve daily and unless we learn strategies and coping skills, we will become overwhelmed and be in a constant state of burnout. Counseling can help a patient put a coping system in place that will enable them to lessen the impact of stress on their condition. This is not to say that all their needs will be met with the learned coping skills, but it will be a great asset to them. Knowing how to relax, focus, and use our faith as somewhat of a "cushion," if you will, is a great asset for anyone.

Dr. Matthews says, "Depression and anxiety are not just in your head, they are real diseases, with physical, emotional, and spiritual pain accompanying well-defined changes in brain chemistry." Anti-depressant medications like Prozac, Zoloft, and Paxil, as well as anti-anxiety drugs like Xanax and Klonopin have made these illnesses much easier to treat. As with prescribed medication for depression or anxiety disorders, good nutrition and regular exercise significantly help in recovery.

Our physical as well as mental health requires rest, relaxation, and inner peace for a time, to allow us to take inventory of our lives and where we are now. Periodically we need to evaluate what we are doing, how we feel, to gauge or measure improvement, changes, or needs. Time alone or one on one with God is a "must do" in our lives.

People need to know it is easy to talk to God and how much pleasure and joy He gets out of our communicating with Him. Guess what, He isn't going to correct your grammar, won't be looking for hidden messages (because He already knows your heart and agenda), and He won't be looking for ways to put you down or trip you up. You need no special form or fashion, just talk to Him. He wants you to spend time with Him. There are times we need to be reminded of this fact.

Counseling can help people come more and more to the realization that they need to pray, read God's word, and to include Him more in their lives. Some have reached this conclusion through problems, illness, frustrations in life, or just a sense of needing more meaning and purpose. The more they reach out to God, the more they realize the benefit of doing so. A sense of support, comfort, and love is what they say they experience when they get closer to God.

Most health problems can involve discomfort or pain; they can cause disability, changes in lifestyle, or they can have the potential to be terminal. The average person would assume the worst when a doctor says that a biopsy must be done, or a condition could be cancerous. Their thoughts will immediately be of death. Their emotions run rampant for a bit, and they need to be calmed down (or even sedated).

Christians who have a solid relationship with the Lord and understand that death is a part of life don't get engulfed in fear. They may feel that they want to leave their loved ones (spouse or children), prepared and cared for, but their own concerns are between them and the Lord. When they are aware of the scriptures, they know that Jesus has prepared a place for their eternal home, meaning never having to move again, ever! They will not spend countless hours as those unsaved will, fearing and emotionally falling apart.

Emotional stress, fear, and worry during a serious condition inhibits the healing of the body. Stress slows up the progress of restoration to wholeness. Part of the reason for this is the fact that it robs the body of rest and sleep it needs, but it also causes the body to deplete nutrients and vital minerals faster. That is why some doctors recommend that supplemental sources be increased during the healing process of some conditions. Some illnesses such as the flu, colds, cancer and surgery often need more vitamins, minerals, or antioxidants to reinforce the body's immune and strength system. The nervous system responds to stress and can add to the negativity of the body's functioning properly.

During the recovery process a patient sometimes consumes far more pain medication than is actually needed. The use of medication inappropriately is adding yet another problem for the patient. Stress intensifies or magnifies the pain level, causing a person to think, "I still need help with this pain." In situations where the patient is on pain medicine that will cause them to be drowsy or sleepy, they may want to keep using the medication to escape the stress or worry they are experiencing. All substance or medication abusers don't use to get high, they may abuse to avoid pain or worry. Actually, stress management training can be taught to them to help with the stress, and once the stress level is eased, the patient may experience less intense pain, which in turn allows them to lower or reduce the frequency of pill taking. Pain medication can be at least reduced in dosage if they learn to focus and use some visualization or imagery techniques.

Prayer for healing has been in existence since the days of the beginning, in the scriptures or biblical times. If there was no result or benefit of praying for healing, it would not have continued from that time until today. Those who fail to pray are those who have disconnected from God, or those who never knew Him, or those who just don't believe in Him. Then there are those that may feel they don't have a right to ask God's blessings, because they feel unworthy or they let Him down. Some feel ashamed for backsliding or have shut God out because they are angry at Him.

James 5:13–15 says, "Is anyone among you sick? Let him call for the elders of the church, and let them pray over him, anointing him with oil in the name of the Lord. And the prayer of faith will save the sick, and the Lord will raise him up." Here once again is where Christian counseling can be of use in the treatment of a patient. This is something most physicians will not attempt to do themselves. But with a team approach that would include a counselor this is a possibility.

Most people acknowledge prayer is a natural or good thing; in other words, it is not unusual or considered weird. It is easy to pray, if you are a believer, because you simply talk to God as someone you know and trust. You can pray openly, in a prayer closet, or silently. However you do it does not matter, so long as you do pray. Counselors should explain to the patient that praying to God and requesting healing is the first sense of comfort and help for them when they become ill. It gives them the feeling that they are not in this alone and they are going to get well.

God is no respecter of persons and He hears the petitions of the believers who seek His blessings upon them. Counseling can help clear up misconceptions about God, healing, and fears. Some people think they can't pray eloquently enough or elaborately, so they want someone with lots of education to pray for them. Nothing could be farther from the truth.

Centuries ago there were plenty of uneducated people who not only prayed themselves, but they led many to Christ. They witnessed endlessly and actually taught others about Christ, using whatever means possible to share about the goodness of the Lord. In some rural areas there were even ministers that had little or no education and even had to get others to read the scriptures to the congregation. But they had a message for their members at every service, a message about God, from God. They knew how to pray and preach.

The areas of counseling to the sick are many and they are all areas of need that others on the medical team/staff will not or do not feel adequate or comfortable addressing. They will acknowledge that it is a real need, but it falls into somewhat of a gray area for them or makes them feel uneasy handling it.

The devil would have us all believe that we are inadequate, we don't have a purpose, we don't fit in the big scheme of things, we have to make it totally on our own, and we are too weak to survive. Satan's plan is to destroy every aspect of our being. If you don't know why, I'll tell you . . . simply because he hates us for being a part of God's divine plan. He knows that God plans to uniquely use us and (unlike him), God loves us deeply.

Counseling is not just for those who are considered mentally ill or seriously disturbed, which is what a lot of people think. Counseling goes from one area of a person's life to the very far end of their life (i.e., family issues, marriage, job, relationships, adjustments, finances, spiritual matters, personal health, etc.), but we must keep an open mind and not allow ourselves to be intimidated by stigmas that have been attached to counseling. Counseling may help a multitude of conditions or situations, but prayer helps everything. Prayer connects us directly to God, our Father.

Most of us are familiar with the idea or concept that the unknown is something to be feared or dreaded. Scientist Marie Curie stated "Nothing in life is to be feared. It is only to be understood." But there are some who find the unknown to be exciting, challenging, or even stimulating. Most explorers or researchers live for the opportunity to examine or study those things unknown. Fear is not of God and it has been said that the only thing to fear is fear itself. Fear can be devastating and it can hold severe consequences if not handled appropriately. Fear in illness is a stressor for the ill.

Illness is not something we enjoy and it is not something we want to prolong by any means. In fact, most conditions get worse if not treated immediately and some sicknesses can become a threat to our lives (i.e., cancer or other serious complications might develop). We need to be proactive when it comes to our health and wellness. It's up to us to take the first step in the restoration of our health, and our mental and spiritual health is equally important.

The human mind can become lax and lose strength to function just as any other part of a person. We need to nurture, care for, and enhance our mental capacity, so it can perform and benefit us at its maximum potential. Counseling helps rid us of health-depriving factors, such a anxiety, stress, worry, and negative overloading. Our thoughts set a trend for our mindset or view of things, such as our potential for healing, or even coping with sickness and disease.

Our mind is like the silly putty that children play with to make or shape things. Our ideas, concepts, and comprehensions of our condition are based on what we understand, knowledge given us, and our emotional endurance. We must use all tools available to us to deal with pressures, illnesses, and our way to recovery. We cannot allow our mind to be shaped by those things that are of no benefit to us spiritually, physically, mentally, or emotionally. We know that fear, worry, and anxiety are not of the Lord; therefore, they are of no value, but have some very negative consequences.

Doctors for many years scratched their heads about patients who had repeated occurrences of certain illnesses, uncontrolled blood pressure problems, psychosomatic illnesses, and general physical weakness. The doctors repeatedly instructed the patient on the importance of good pressure levels, the need for diet and exercise, controlling stress, etc. They felt the patient just didn't care or were in heavy denial about the seriousness of it all. The poor doctors did what they are trained to do, but they failed to realize that counseling would be of great benefit to the patient. They needed more than the medical component. Overlooking the faith and prayer components doesn't help, and the psychology pulls in the whole screen or view of things, if included. It is like giving the patient partial doses of medicine and expecting healing.

In keeping with the need to holistically treat the mind,

body, and the soul, we must keep with the mindset that health care should include all three. It is when we try to deny this approach that we find the patient's benefit from treatment to be less than what it could be. It is the patient that isn't given the treatment of their whole being who will be one who has the attitude of discouragement. They will feel uncertain about tomorrow or get the "difficult patient syndrome." At some point they will be unable to hide their feelings of despair well. "A man without self control is as defenseless as a city with broken down walls" (Proverbs 25:28).

Dr. David Stoop, Ph.D., author of *You Are What You Think,* states, "Attitude is everything!" Just about every motivational speaker underlines this message. Apostle Paul emphasized the importance of our attitude when he wrote, "Now your attitudes and thoughts must all be constantly changing for the better" (Ephesians 4:23).

Life's problems and woes are directly linked to the millions of people being ill today. The strain from pressures, loss of sleep, poor eating habits, and relationship problems all unite forces with negative thoughts and attitudes to ignite flames of illness and health crises. I believe that counseling with medical treatment can curtail some of the problems that may occur during the course of the patient's illness. The person is already over-burdened with issues that cause the illness and those same issues serve to actually complicate or prolong the illness.

Dr. Stoop states that "Because of chaos and stress, many of us end up not feeling well. Over 40 million Americans suffer from allergies; and 30 million suffer from sleep-onset insomnia. It's estimated that 24 million people in the United States are afflicted with hypertension (high blood pressure). Around 20 million of us have ulcers, and too many millions suffer from jagged nerves to the point of needing tranquilizers. And more than that, one out of three persons has a weight problem, creating unhealthy cycles of weight loss and gain."

We all can take inventory of our own health and illnesses, and then consider what problems we may be experiencing. If we really think about it, we can realize what was going on in our lives at the time our symptoms began. We are affected by our attitudes about our life problems and issues we feel we have no control over. If we would get into counseling at the time of the arrival of the symptoms (really before the symptoms), we would save ourselves a lot of trouble and pain.

Dr. Don Colbert, M.D., in his book, *What You Don't Know May Be Killing You*, says that "how you feel in your heart can show in your body. The two are more powerfully connected than you actually realize." We can do an assessment of our habits, lifestyles, and our emotional status and make changes to improve and enhance our overall well-being. When we continue on in stressful conditions or ways and neglect to add relaxation, stress relief, and prayer, we multiply our chances of becoming sick and disease-ridden.

A counselor can help with evaluating your areas to modify, and recommend methods to address them through relaxation, rest, schedule reformation, and the elimination of problem areas. It is very helpful to be objective and to have a definite goal in mind when we seek to make changes for the better in our lives. We must define our goals clearly and seek to meet the criteria set to help achieve them. We must attempt to be at ease during this process. Being at ease allows you to be comfortable with yourself and to reflect on the negatives you want to conquer and the positives you want to achieve.

A closer look at counseling those who are ill will reveal that the more serious the illness, the more treatment and more people to be involved in the patient's care. Recovery time is longer for those who are seriously ill as well. During the treatment and recovery the patient has a lot of time to think, worry, and wonder about their prognosis. Guess what else is going on; the old serpent is raising his ugly, evil head, with all sorts of tricks and antics. After all, he is the enemy of all mankind. He will be planting seeds of doubt, fear, anxiety, anger, and all sorts of mind games and negativity.

The best recourse to warding off the enemy is to have spiritual support and counseling for the patient as part of the treatment. God did not give us the spirit of fear because He only gives us good things that will benefit us, and He promised not to put on us more than we can bear. The devil attacks the mind, which in turn affects our physical well-being. Therefore, we must build up and strengthen the mind and control our emotions.

We have already established that emotional problems or concerns will hinder a patient's healing and recovery. We also know that because the mind and body are working together, what affects one obviously affects the other. There are many seriously ill people that have had so much pain, fear, doubt, and feelings of hopelessness, they have committed suicide. Mostly because they saw no other way out of pain and did not want to be a burden to loved ones. Some were dealing with cancer, serious heart or kidney conditions, or permanent paralysis, Parkinson's disease, or Alzheimer's disease.

Most people assume that those who commit suicide are non-Christians, but that is not always the case, some are. This is what some call a lack of faith or just plain giving up. In all fairness we should look a little closer at what could have made a big difference in that person's situation.

By placing a counselor in with this patient from the very beginning (at the time of diagnosis), the seriously ill patient would have professional, emotional support and encouragement in faith. They would have someone to pray with them from the very onset, someone to motivate them and be a spiritual coach, if you will. They would have someone to guide and support them through each stage, as needed.

The counseling concept in regards to medical treatment has not taken on like wild fire, but awareness of its need is growing. Part of the hesitation is due to the medical doctors only seeing their obligation as being of a medical nature to the patient. They see their duties as addressing the physical aspect only. They feel that the patient and their family should seek out any additional care or services needed. But the doctor can actually fully treat the patient if the cause of the illness is eradicated. Treating that current problem only will allow others to just manifest in the patient because the source is still there.

Concern for a patient's well-being should be at the forefront for the caregivers, relatives, and all involved. All necessary services and types of assistance should be offered or made available. When suggesting or offering counseling services, the patient and their immediate family (spouse/parent), should raise questions or voice concerns at the time. The physician or counselor can then clarify the benefits of including counseling in the patient's treatment.

I feel it is all a matter of presentation whether or not a person accepts something new or different, such as counseling as a part of a medical treatment program. If the physicians and other medical providers are enthusiastic and supportive of the concept when they explain the need and benefits of counseling in medicine, the patient will be more receptive to its use. But the physicians must be open-minded and accepting of it themselves first. You can't sell a product that you yourself don't believe in or like. It would be like an atheist working in a Christian bookstore or a church school, it won't work!!

People who have concerns about worrying relatives or being a burden will not let them know how worried they are themselves. A good example of this would be a patient who needs a heart bypass surgery performed. They will not share their fears about the surgery with their spouse or other loved one, they may admit to being a little nervous, but that's it. In actuality, they are terrified or at least scared for themselves. They may fear death or some serious complication, such as blood clots or undue bleeding.

Another case example could be a patient who has to have breast cancer surgery. A lot of things will be going through her mind and at the top of the list would be how her spouse (or future spouse) will feel about how her body will look after surgery. She'll wonder if it will return and how the chemotherapy and radiation will possibly affect her. She will have fear that she has never had before. The doctor or nurse will undoubtedly not have time nor feel adequate to counsel her in these matters. They can only be sympathetic and try to reassure her.

The two above scenarios are just two examples of how counseling the seriously ill patient is needed. Counselors can address their fear as well as address their faith, pray and offer assistance in areas of planning for community services that they may need. The patient can confidentially share their deeper concerns with the counselor and not feel they are a burden to relatives. They may need help in their communicating with God, and this would be especially true if they aren't currently a member of a local church or married to an unsaved spouse.

Medically speaking, the contemplation of major surgery or the diagnosis of a debilitating illness will cause anxiety and stress, and the potential for depression is very real. This is not unusual by any means; in fact, some doctors say it is a part of the territory. The stress and anxiety will heighten the pain or take their nerves to another scale or level. Patients are not to be clumped in a bunch and be expected to all respond the same, therefore, we need to be prepared to provide what they need, according to their individual responses to their illness.

Patients don't always have coping skills and those they do have may not be appropriate (i.e., drinking, drugs, overeating). Counseling can help a patient in learning and using coping skills. There are times in our lives that we have more difficulty surviving or dealing with issues we are confronted with, but we have to learn to deal with them in a positive and beneficial manner. The word "cope" is defined as to contend with difficulties and to overcome them successfully.

Coping skills allow us not to add to the stress we are already experiencing. In fact, these skills are used to help relieve tensions or stress. We put skills in place to minimize the effects of stress, or eliminate extreme pressure that can be internalized and cause physical problems. Coping can be done successfully when we learn and practice relaxation techniques. Learning skills to cope is never a waste of time.

It is not just during illness that coping skills can be used. These skills can be used when you are encountering more stress than usual, or just to unwind or relax from a hard day's work. These are skills we can use at any time during our life. Sometimes we just need to plan a "care session," to treat our body, mind, and spirit to a mini spa. We all occasionally need to reward ourselves and pamper our inner selves and spirits.

Dr. Alice D. Domar, Ph.D., author of *Healing Mind, Healthy Woman,* states that mind body medicine is "any method in which we use our minds to change our behavior or physiology in order to promote health and recovery from illness."

Dr. Domar says this process would include the following:

1. Any technique that elicits a state of relaxation, such as meditation, yoga, mindfulness, and deep breathing.
2. "Cognitive therapy" on an individual and group basis. This approach, which helps us to challenge and replace thought patterns that make us depressed and anxious, has been shown to enhance physical as well as psychological health.
3. The teaching of coping skills, such as self-nurturing, seeking support, problem solving, emotional expression, and journaling which are effective forms of stress management.
4. Assertiveness training and communication skills that empower us to develop and sustain a nurturing network of relationships.
5. Biofeedback and hypnosis, which tap mental capacities to conditions such as irritable bowel syndrome, migraine headaches, and many other conditions.
6. If you have small children, arrange ahead of time for their care or be sure they are otherwise occupied.
7. Find a regular time of day to elicit the relaxation response. If you miss that regular time for this, make it up the same day, even if it's just some time before bedtime to practice relaxation.

8. You can elicit the relaxation response in any comfortable position. However, sitting is generally preferred, primarily because you are less likely to drift off into sleep than if lying down.

9. A single session for eliciting the relaxation response generally lasts between fifteen and twenty-five minutes. If you are particularly stressed out or simply want to deepen your practice, you can certainly benefit by eliciting the relaxation response twice a day.

I know many people say that their schedules are too hectic to formally incorporate relaxation time, but many people don't even look their schedule over, to see if it is adjustable. Just twenty to thirty minutes could add health and years to their life.

Operating from a negative perspective will cause increased stress when we use negative emotions to handle difficult situations. We lack the support of a sound foundation (unsure footing), when we allow our negativity to cloud our judgment. We should avoid falling prey to resentment, guilt, suppressed anger, and anxiety, if at all possible, because they will just defeat our efforts to resolve the situation in a positive manner.

In her book, *The Total De-Stress Plan,* author Beth MacEoin states that "Although some of us may feel uncomfortable with anger as an emotion, it is important to recognize that in its appropriate place, justifiably expressed anger can be a positive, liberating experience, burning up grievances and hurts. Letting go of any negative feelings we may have been carrying around from the past leaves us free to enjoy the present."

Five major sections of de-stressing:

1. Calm
2. Nurture
3. Replenish
4. Pamper
5. Rebalance

Calm is self-explanatory or self-defined, if you will. It means without disturbance, tranquil, non-chaotic, at peace, relaxed . . . no waves. We must use mental and emotional techniques from our inner selves to relieve stress.

Nourish is caring for ourselves nutritionally, eliminating foods, supplements, and substances that may influence our susceptibility to stress (healthy habits and diets).

Replenish is to restore or build up; to calm the mind, emotions, and spirit; to re-energize yourself using healthful means or activities.

Pamper is to gently care for yourself, to focus on relaxing, healing, and nurturing yourself . . . a time just for you to be priority #1, yourself for a time.

Rebalance is treating yourself to improve the quality of your overall being, such as your physical, emotional, and spiritual sides, through alternative treatments or medicines (natural).

In times of need and especially during illness, we cannot go through the process alone. Even a simple case of the flu is a time we want some caring persons there for us. The average person does have a support unit in place at most times. But that is not always the case. Some people go it alone in times of illness.

A patient that has an illness that will require surgery or needs some extensive treatment, needs some support in place. They will need support that affords them the time and opportunity to heal and mend physically. Each situation or person may have very different needs. The support team will need to be in one accord, with the same goal for the patient. Their primary goal is to provide the necessary services and assistance to the patient.

We are now in very different times than generations before us. We are dealing with family compositions and makeup, totally different from the past. There are more single parent households and people are opting to stay single longer before marrying and to have children. There are those who are married, but due to their being in the military, they are not in their hometown area. Other folk may have accepted jobs in other areas of the country and don't know anyone in the immediate area well. But as we all know, medical sickness doesn't always happen at the most opportune times. This is when a support team has to be created and a counselor can be the beginning of this process. God, the physician, and a counselor is a team that everyone should begin with.

It is devastating to say the least to hear that you have cancer or need heart surgery or an organ transplant. Most people actually feel as though the air has been knocked out of them when the doctor give them such diagnoses. It is difficult to receive this type information regardless of the individual's sex or gender. We know that at any given time we can hear of a loved one or ourselves having a diagnosis "bomb" dropped in your lap. It is not something you welcome.

When we are ill, we are to continue on in prayer and faith, but in addition to that we can use tools to help us remain relaxed so that fear attacks from the enemy do not take hold of us. We need to learn ways to focus, to get and stay calm, and to rest properly during sickness and recovery. Some people like reading Psalms or other soothing scriptures, others listen to soft inspirational music, or quietly praise the Lord.

Dr. Myles Munroe, Ph.D., in his book *Understanding the Power In Prayer* stated the following: "Power in prayer is not based on feelings but on the word of God. His word is the guarantee of answered prayer. God is asking you to bring Him His word, to plead your covenant rights. We are not to pray to God in ignorance, but as partners in His purposes. Prayer is joining forces with God the Father by calling attention to His promises." The best and strongest support anyone can have is the support of God. We need only to go to God in prayer and He'll do the rest!

Three
Making Informed Decisions on Treatment

The first step to making informed decisions is getting the facts. Far too many patients fail to get enough information from their physicians about their conditions. It's not to say that doctors don't try to give information to their patients, it's just that they may not have enough time to allow the patient to ask all the questions or get the clarification they need. Some diagnoses are shocks or totally unexpected and it causes the patient not to focus on anything, but what they just heard. But they need to get all the information they can get.

Patients don't always know to what extent their condition will affect them, the exact prognosis, what alternative treatments are available, what caused their condition, and how to avoid a recurrence. They may want to get a second opinion. There are so many answers they need and their not knowing will just cause a lot of undue stress for them. Doctors do as much as they humanly can to inform and enlighten their patients. But with sometimes being understaffed, huge patient caseloads, hospital rounds, and emergency care, more time just isn't available. This is by no means to say doctors don't do excellent jobs and don't have the best interest of their patients at heart. But patients share the responsibility of their health care and treatment decisions.

Questions from the patient are usually (more often than not), welcomed by the doctor. This avoids confusion on the part of the patient about the serious condition and the accuracy of the information. But the doctor can only answer questions if the patient asks them. Everyone doesn't have the same comprehension or understanding. The only way the doctor knows the patient doesn't understand is if the patient says so. Some medical terminology can be very confusing to anyone, and those who do understand it (such as the doctors), too often assume they have simplified it so that anyone can understand it.

Many illnesses or diseases sound similar in pronunciation and have similar symptoms. In fact, some illnesses have all the same symptoms with only one different symptom. The doctor is the expert or the one to make a sound diagnosis. We need to leave that to them, but if we feel it best to get a second opinion, most doctors don't have any objections or will not consider it insulting to them.

God desires that we not be confused or lack knowledge. We are to seek wisdom and knowledge according to God's word. Proverbs 10:14 states, "Wise people store up knowledge, but the mouth of the foolish is near destruction." Gathering information about your illness makes it easier to understand your condition, your treatment, and the necessity of taking your medication as prescribed as well. It makes us not be vulnerable to the devil trying to cause undue stress and fear over our condition, and he can't put us in "panic" mode with his lies and deceit.

Some people procrastinate about going to the doctor in the first place because of fears. They allow the enemy to pull up thoughts of what ifs and someone else's health issues to scare them. They often allow fears of others' serious illnesses, such as cancer, contagious illness, genetic and hereditary conditions, and other things to allow them to avoid being checked. Actually, that is why they should go, for their own peace of mind, to get timely medical treatment and to rule out the conditions they are afraid of having.

Some people put off going to the doctor so long that the problem is now at advance stages and requires more drastic measures, or is actually now a larger concern than it initially would have been. Knowledge is power and it is always to your advantage to have an abundance of it in regards to illness and your medical treatment. Getting all the facts and getting treatment right away is the only way to assure yourself of the best care and more options in your treatment.

People worry needlessly about health issues that are not considered life threatening or serious. Why? It's simple, they lack the facts about their condition because they won't go to have it checked by the physician. Instead, they worry, use a home remedy for what they think the problem is (yes, even today people use old remedies), or credit it to the fact they have been working too hard or need more rest. God's word says we are to be anxious for nothing. We are to give or cast our cares upon the Lord and trust in Him because He is faithful to His word. Proverbs 13:25 says, "Anxiety in the heart of man causes depression, but a good word makes it glad."

We need facts and details to understand anything we are not familiar with or have not experienced before. It may seem simple to one person, but complex to another, based on their educational level and the ability to comprehend. Sometimes it is assumed by a person with education and expertise in an area that everyone should or can understand the basic facts. Let's face it, everyone has not the same level of education or intellect level. A little knowledge can also be dangerous to some folks. Some people have a little training in an area or have secondhand knowledge or limited experience, but think they are qualified to try to instruct others (wrong thing to do).

There are developments, discoveries in research, and treatment updates daily. Medications change based on those discoveries, giving patients more options from which to select. We don't have to assume that we will have to go through what Aunt Bessie and Grandma went through. So we should not hesitate to see a doctor when we realize that something is going on with our health. Proverbs 15:14 states, "The heart of him who has understanding seeks knowledge, but the mouth of fools feeds on foolishness." Some of our ideas are just that, "foolish thoughts"! Therefore, just because a diabetic relative became a double amputee does not mean you will suffer the same. Unless you have been tested, you may not even be diabetic.

We need to express our concerns, ask questions, and inquire about alternative procedures in reference to treatment for illnesses. Only a doctor can tell the difference between one condition or another, so you must give all of your symptoms of your problem. In the event you still have concerns after giving him the details of your ailment, ask any question you may have until you feel at ease.

Undue stress over health issues just makes more problems and adds to your discomfort. We are not to borrow problems from tomorrow because the devil will try to throw you some today. Most importantly, get counsel in regards to your treatment and medical procedures. Be sure to follow directions on the medicines just as they are prescribed. Be sure to let the doctor know what medications you are on from another physician and ask if they will interact negatively. Adjustments or alternative treatment may have to be made due to possible drug interactions.

Proverbs 15:22, "Without counsel, plans go awry, but in the multitude of counselors they are established." Also in the scripture, Proverbs 11:14, "Where there is no counsel, the people fall; But in the multitude of counselors there is safety." When the patient and the doctor discuss the illness, plan together for the treatment, and the patient fully understands it all, they are both ensuring what is best to achieve a healthy status or be well again. They both need to be on the same page at the same time and in full agreement on each course of action.

We need to take the time and the physicians are required to fully inform the patient of his or her health status and the appropriate treatment, based on the current available treatment options. It is a give and take session, so to speak, when patient and doctor discuss health care options openly and honestly. It is a matter of identifying the best medication and treatment for you.

As a patient, you have the right to the following and you should see that you get it:

1. The doctor should inform you of the medication he plans to prescribe for you and how it works
2. Share any information he has on the clinical testing/safety of that drug or product for treatment
3. Any known side effects of the drug and interaction with other medications you may be taking
4. How long you can safely take the drug and long- or short-term use
5. The potential of the medication being addictive
6. Should or will the doctor do periodic blood work to test for damage control (i.e., liver or muscular damage, etc.)

7. The doctor should be sure to inform the patient of all the necessary facts about the drug or drugs being prescribed

The patient has the key responsibility for informing the doctor of pertinent information about his or her current medications and conditions he or she is being treated for by other physicians. Share concerns or knowledge about any known adverse reactions to medications in the past. There are drugs that have the same main ingredient or are in the same chemical family so to speak (i.e., various codeine-containing drugs, sulfur-containing drugs, etc.). These facts will influence or control your treatment options. By all means take a list of medicines you are currently taking along with you to the doctor's office visit.

Doctors also need to know if you have allergic reactions to any medical supplies or topical solutions. Some people are allergic to iodine solutions, others may be allergic to latex bandages or surgical gloves. It can be lethal for some people to have contact with latex.

People who are allergic to seafood are also allergic to iodine tincture solutions application as well. For your own safety, these are things that you need to be sure to inform your doctor about.

Following what I am sharing and suggesting to you can help eliminate any uneasiness you may have and enable you to fully exercise the treatment options available to you. In addition to your sharing information with the doctor, here is where the give and take come in. You need to be sure to get more information, beyond what they have already shared with you, if necessary. A patient cannot ask too many questions; if you feel the need for clarification, remember it's your health and your life here. Here is a list of things that are appropriate and acceptable to ask your physician:

1. How will I know if the medication needs to be changed? (Believe it or not some people may need to ask this question because some drugs may not show the desired results, and a more effective drug may be needed.)
2. Ask them to repeat how to take the medication properly and if it matters if it is taken with, before, or after meals. This does make a difference in some medications' ability to work. The pharmacist indicates on the bottle instructions as to how to use medications. But there are still some folk unable to read well.
3. Will this drug cause drowsiness, sleeplessness, or make me jittery? Most of the time you are told this, but if you are not aware, this could be a problem for you in reference to driving, caring for small children, or getting enough sleep to function or make sound or safe decisions.
4. Are there foods or drinks that you need to avoid while taking the medication? There are foods or liquids that prevent the medicine from working affectively (i.e., dairy products will interfere with antibiotics working and grapefruit or its juice will cause some medications not to work appropriately).
5. There are many health-conscious people today that take herb supplements. They need to let the doctor know what those are and how they take them, as well as why they take them. Herbs can interact with drugs or can cause what is considered "free" or heavy bleeding, or other significant problems.
6. Inquire about the cost of medications if that is a

concern for you, if you are on a fixed income, or need to watch your finances closely. Your doctor may even know if your insurance will cover certain medications. Why am I adding this concern in with this information? Because some people leave a doctor's office and due to inability to afford the drug prescribed, wait several days or weeks before they can get the medicine. In the meantime, the condition is getting worse or complications set in. When actually a simple solution could have been to ask if he could prescribe or indicate approval for a generic drug in place of the name brand. Due to being ashamed (pride, which is a sin), or failing to exercise your option of a generic drug, the patient will suffer the consequences. Generic is definitely the option for the patient who has no health insurance coverage.

Let us move on to options to consider besides medication for the patient. Surgical options, selecting types of anesthesia to be used during surgery, alternative treatment method, the selection of a surgical facility, post-operative care, and pain management.

Believe it or not, the medical profession is now allowing the patient to have more input and offering options for you to decide upon. This comes at a time that they are now looking more positively at including prayer, faith, and spirituality as a part of the treatment for health care (praise the Lord). For too long the physicians made these decisions for their patients. They basically told the patient the plan of action for their care and treatment. Your opinions and concerns do matter and voicing them to the doctors can result in less stress and worry for you.

Hospitals are becoming just as competitive as other institutions and organizations. Basically, there are more hospitals in our cities and towns today. When I was growing up, we had only three in my city and those hospitals were segregated, with only one that accepted non-white patients. You had no say at all which one to go to and what treatment you could get. We were fortunate, though, because some rural areas had no nearby hospitals, and many people had to travel miles for treatment.

This is another area of having no options or choice, because women who had babies in those rural areas had no options. Their babies were delivered by the midwives nearby and they prayed the whole time that there would be no complications during their delivery. The people who needed emergency surgery or were in auto accidents did not always make it to the hospitals in time. Sad to say, but there were no options.

Hospitals today advertise on television and in the newspapers. They let it be known that they have some of the best or newest technological equipment available in the area, comparing themselves to other local hospitals. They may say they have the only space-age MRI or CATSCAN equipment, or they boast about the best heart surgeon or the latest in cancer treatment programs available today. I could go on and on about their media advertisement, but the bottom line is that patients are afforded more options, more say, or input, and more updated facilities to use.

For pain management and anesthesia we have more choices today than in previous years. Some doctors now offer as a courtesy to their patients the opportunity to talk to the anesthesiologist before their surgery. This enables the patient to feel a little more at ease, and have input as to what type of pain management or type of anesthesia they personally prefer.

An anesthesiologist is a medically trained person who has attended college and medical school and did an internship and residency. They work with a care team during your surgery that consists of themselves, a nurse, your surgeon, and a peri-operative nurse. They are each professionally trained in their respective area of study. There are more than a couple of types of anesthesia. I will give you a brief bit of information on the various types offered for treatment or use.

Anesthesia is a local or general insensibility to pain with or without the loss of consciousness induced by partial or total loss of sensation, and may be topical, local, regional, or general, depending on the method of administration and the area of the body affected.

1. Local anesthesia is the application of an anesthetic to a focal area and typically does not involve an anesthesiologist.
2. Monitored Anesthesia Care (MAC), is local anesthesia plus a sedative, which involves an anesthesiologist.
3. General Anesthesia is a drug-induced loss of consciousness during which patients are not able to be aroused. Early general anesthesia was administered by dripping anesthesia to a sponge and draping it over the patient's nose. But the modern method allows a regulated administration of anesthesia during the surgical procedure. During this time the anesthesiologist is monitoring your safety.
4. Regional Anesthesia is the loss of sensation in a region of the body produced by application of an anesthesia agent to all the nerves in that region. Early regional techniques were spinal and

epidural. The latest regional techniques are nerve blocks, which are used to reduce or eliminate pain with fewer side effects for the patient.

The advantages of blocks are as follows:

1. The ability to avoid general anesthesia and subsequently avoid the post-operative nausea and vomiting
2. They avoid the risk of pulmonary complications
3. Better pain control for days
4. Faster recovery
5. Quicker return home
6. Can be used with other methods as well

Disadvantages of blocks are as follows:

1. Failed blocks
2. Bleeding avoidance for patients who are anticoagulated (blood thinner)
3. Infection (very rare)
4. Injury to nerves

I'm sure by now you are wondering why am I going into so much detail about surgical information. I am doing so not because I think you are interested in pre-medicine, or that I am, but because these are the things you need to know and should ask about prior to surgery. I am talking about you having the right to make choices. Knowing your options and making them in an informed manner. I want you to ask questions about your medical treatment and know how these treatments are going to affect you and which one is best for you.

It is my desire that you as a patient step up to the plate

and get involved with the decision-making process of your treatment procedures. Whatever is decided directly affects your healing and recovery process. We need to be less in the dark about these things and more at ease or relaxed, so that stress is not a hindrance to our well-being.

As for your treatment and care and the law, all patients have the right to adequate analgesia and pain management. A pain assessment should be performed often, a therapeutic plan and goal of analgesia should be assessed for each patient, and the state and federal law mandates that health care professionals treat pain adequately.

Knowledge is powerful, but the knowledge doesn't have to be of "super science" level. Just knowing some basic, but very important health treatment facts can make you more comfortable, and it may even save your life. We today are always seeking to improve or at least maintain our health at a maximum level.

Four

Appropriate Use of Prescribed Medication

In chapter one we covered what causes illness and the need for including prayer and faith. Three of the main causes of illness, as I mentioned in the first chapter, are stress, tension, and worry. Chester L. Tolson, Ph.D., and Harold G. Koenig, M.D., stated that "stress may be caused by environment, personality, mental attitudes, or events occurring around you." Some of these factors are beyond our control. We can, however, control how we react to the stressors in our lives.

People usually allow stress overload because they are in denial that something can happen to them. But it is very important that they practice ways to manage their stress because stress not only can cause your illnesses, but it can also interfere in healing and recovery. The culprit, stress, goes a step further and can intensify your pain. Thus, the need for pain medication can be prolonged or dosage amounts may need to be increased.

We would not have to resort to putting medications into our bodies, nor would we have a need for pain management if we kept our bodies as the temple they are meant to be. God gave us healthy and nutritious foods to eat and He told us to cast our cares upon Him. If we did that, we would not have the sicknesses that we experience today.

According to DrugItel's website, 106,000 people in the United States die each year from adverse reactions to medication. These are not illegal drugs, either. These are the drugs manufactured by legitimate pharmaceutical companies, prescribed by licensed medical doctors, and approved by the FDA. On top of this, another 7,000 people die each year because of hospital errors in administering drugs!

Dr. Cris Enriquez, M.D. says, "The irony of ironies: Drugs designed to help people get better become one of the most common causes of death." It is astonishing to think that even with the best of intentions and in the best of hands, something so common can become so fatal.

Think health maintenance, and don't merely try to heal or to get well after illness happens. We know that actually the vast majority of all sicknesses can be avoided or at least kept to a minimum. With the practice of a healthy lifestyle, eating well, minimizing stress, and maintaining a sound relationship with the Lord, we can experience more wholeness or better health. God gave us our bodies as temples for the Holy Ghost, not disease and pain. "Do you not know that your body is the temple of the Holy Spirit who is in you, whom you have from God, and you are not your own?" (I Corinthians 6:19) (NKJV).

Those of you who doubt the effect of stress on your health need to pay more attention to health news programs or just carefully read your daily newspapers. It is easy to learn about the things that we need to know to benefit us. An article in my local paper dated February 10, 2005, had the following health information and facts: Doctors began treating a woman for what they thought was a heart attack. But the woman's arteries were fine, so the doctor and his colleagues subsequently determined instead that she had experienced an unusual heart malfunction. She quickly recovered. Stress can initiate many physical malfunctions. Researchers have known for a long time that stress could trigger heart attacks in people prone to them.

Herbert Benson, a mind-body researcher at Harvard says, "Stress must be viewed as a disease-causing entity."

It is imperative that we begin to realize what makes us sick and what we can do to avoid illness. We have to understand that medications are not the solution and they can add to our physical problems. Drug side effects can be worse than the illness you are taking it for. "An ounce of prevention is worth more than a pound of cure," as they say. If we prevent illness, we can avoid putting medication into our body.

Dr. Enriquez says that "in medical practice, there is an old adage, probably derived from the Hippocratic oath, which says, first, do no harm." I am certain that most physicians have this in mind when they treat patients. They do the best they can to heal and not harm. In the use of prescription drugs, however, side effects and adverse reactions frequently do develop, which have the potential of doing harm.

We all have been seeing advertising and reports of very harmful prescription drugs that have proven to be harmful. Some have caused heart attacks, strokes, paralysis, or even death in some.

Some of the drugs that have been previously considered safe are being reviewed, questioned, or even being considered to be taken off the market are Celebrex, Vioxx, and Mobic. These are all pain pills that are usually prescribed for arthritis patients. The Food and Drug Administration (FDA) is the government agency with the responsibility of checking out the safety of drugs for marketing approval. It is also the agency that can have medications pulled from the market for the safety of persons using these medicines. There are drugs that come under scrutiny and criticism after patients have suffered negative reactions or serious side effects from the use of them.

Medications are given for healing and or pain relief. We are to use them as instructed and monitor how they affect us during the use of them. We are not to assume that physical changes or new symptoms are caused or based on our surgery or illness. We are responsible for notifying our physician right away if any new symptoms develop, or our conditions get worse.

Examples of some side effects are:

1. Severe headache
2. Stomach pain
3. Severe back or leg pain
4. Severe nausea
5. Black or bloody vomit or stool
6. Unusual weakness or dizziness or irregular heartbeat
7. Weakness in wrist or fingers
8. Weight loss/loss of appetite
9. Dramatic change in output
10. Yellow eyes or skin, or a rash

The complications from using a medication can outweigh the benefit of using them for your condition. Some people feel they're safe taking whatever their doctor prescribes for them, simply because a doctor tells them to use it and the FDA has said it is safe for human consumption. Why not think that whatever the doctor recommends is safe, they are trained to do so.

Joan Mathews Larson, Ph.D., author of *7 Weeks to Emotional Healing,* says "Drugs should be avoided whenever possible because they are toxic and cause many worrisome side effects." Certain prescription drugs are well-known for causing depression. According to a 1993 British medical journal, the following prescription drugs cause depression:

1. Heart medications
2. Blood pressure medications (i.e., diuretics and calcium channel blockers
3. Estrogen replacement therapies
4. Sleeping pills
5. Benzodiazepines

Dr. Larson goes on to say, "It is imperative that you examine the dates of your prescription medication(s) in conjunction with your onset of depression symptoms."

Prescribed medications come in many classifications, categories, and levels of effectiveness. Some can be addictive, while others are not classified as addictive.

No one starts the use of any drug or substance with the intent or goal of becoming dependent or addicted. It takes time to become dependent on a drug. An example of this is the use of the pain medications Percocet, Vicodin, and opiates. These drugs have to be used quite a while to become addictive.

The doctor knows how long it should take for the patient to recover from their illness or surgery. They know or have an approximate idea of how long excruciating or debilitating pain should last. Persistent pain could indicate infection, re-injury, or some other complications. The doctor may give a few more pills, just enough to allow the patient time to get testing or evaluation to see why they are still experiencing pain. But using the pills should be a short-lived period of time.

Being prepared for surgery or lengthy illnesses emotionally, mentally, and spiritually will allow the patient to heal and use medication appropriately. It takes the mind and emotions of a person to work cohesively to attain a level of acceptance and willingness to work with the doctors.

We need to use prayer, faith, and focus to limit the use of pain medications. Some people who overuse drugs or feel that they need an extension of their prescription usually have some other things going on. Some just need to draw more on their faith and put God in charge of their circumstances. People need to be obedient to God's word and instruction, and follow His guidance, as well as following their doctor's care instructions.

Doctors who don't see the need to have counseling involved in the treatment of the patient do not see the correlation between the inappropriate use of medications and the underlying problems of the patient. They could feel that they are there to treat the medical ills of the person, no more and no less. But when they see their patient continually request pain medication, or that the person's condition is not getting better, or new health issues keep surfacing, it's time to consider underlying causes of their illness.

All doctors know and understand the definition of "psychosomatic," yet they still treat the physical symptoms with medication and move on. They cannot do much more than that on their own, and timewise that is understandable. Patients handling their stress, frustrations, and problems by taking sleep-inducing drugs are the ones who are inappropriately using their medications. It is a known fact that people tend to want to mask their problems however they can. They want to escape dealing with issues they prefer not to handle. They will use sickness as an excuse not to face an issue on the job, or handle difficult personal matters.

Medications can become a crutch of sorts for some

people. They use it to do more than ease the pain. It can allow them to get attention from someone they feel neglected by, they may use it to sleep, thus avoiding their emotional pain or hurt (medicines that cause sleepiness or drowsiness). Such behavior is considered an inappropriate use of medication.

There are other ways of using medication incorrectly, such as adding medicines prescribed for other people along with the one prescribed for you, or adding over-the-counter or alternative herbal treatments to the prescribed medications. These can be serious combinations and could possibly be lethal. We need to inform our primary physician of anything we decided to do that alters the treatment plan given by them. We need their approval.

There are ways that a person can do serious harm to themselves through their medication, when used to address their underlying issues. The person who is dealing with other personal problems that are not medical can be misusing their medications because of those issues. Some of these issues could be marital, financial, behavioral problems of children, no support from others during their illness, worry concerning job issues, etc.

People in the above-mentioned situations could possibly skip a dose of medicine, then when they realize it, they take it too close to the next scheduled dose, thus causing a possible overdose or another negative reaction. They could mistake how much medication to take because drug instructions have different amounts to take and some should be taken every four hours, while others are to be taken every six hours. One medicine you're to take two tablets and another one requires that you take one capsule. The patients with issues of concern do not willfully or intentionally abuse or misuse their medications. They are doing the

54

best that they can under their particular circumstances. They may reverse the doses of the two.

The financial circumstances of some patients may cause them to not begin taking the medication on time, which prolongs the beginning of the healing process. Lack of money could cause them to try to stretch the medicine by taking only half doses at a time. Some people are prescribed medicines and another family member becomes ill with similar symptoms and they share the medicine. But remember I mentioned earlier that some illnesses have some of the same symptoms and only one symptom could be different, which means they may not have the same illness. Sharing medicine is never a good idea because even if the illnesses are the same, the doctor only prescribed enough to treat one person fully.

Antibiotics are drugs you cannot share with others. The doctor tells the patient to take the antibiotic until it is all gone because it takes the full amount to clear up and avoid the return of a bacterial infection. So sharing it is not an option at any time.

It would do a world of good for patients to be allowed the opportunity to talk to a counselor during illness and in the preparation for surgery to address the things that may become a hindrance to healing and recovery. Those potential stressors are going to become evident at some point during their treatment and care. Why not afford them the opportunity to address stress head on, to avoid for them the difficulty of healing or delayed recovery?

Knowing that faith in God is their hope in healing and that He cares for them, patients should combine prayer, faith, and medication as their formula to attain wholeness again. Healing is the process of transitioning to soundness or the wholeness God intended us to live in. We must always keep the body, mind, and spirit connected for functionnig at our fullest capacity level and potential. It is important that the patient get their priorities in order first, then prepare to face the challenge of healing. All the counselors in the world can't do what God alone can do to equip the patient to deal with issues and illnesses. Therefore, it is imperative that patients have a real relationship with God and trust in his every promise. It is vital that they have a prayer relationship with God. We cannot emphasize enough the power of God and the role He wants to play or be in our lives. He takes precedence over all other sources or efforts we use in our life.

> "In our spiritual lives we believe in a power outside of ourselves, greater than ourselves. Through a relationship with a spiritual Higher Power we learn to perceive and accept a natural order, a natural flow. We learn to see the important space we inhabit within the world among other living beings, but we also learn that we're only one piece of humanity. We also develop a relationship we can turn to when family and friends are not enough or can't be there for some reason. We learn to believe in and trust something greater than ourselves."

Dr. Abraham J. Twerski, M.D., made the above statement about the importance of a relationship with a Higher Power and the benefit of faith and trust in our lives. He says that "we can believe and trust that there will be future moments of serenity and a sense of well-being." Dr. Twerski is a medical doctor and the author of *Addictive Thinking, Addictive Personality.*

We must use our faith and medication to achieve wholeness, but we must let those with the abilities we don't have make this a reality. We must call on those with those abilities and do so in the right protocol. We must, above all things and first, call on God, even before we make an appointment to see the doctor. We pray to God that we will be delivered from the illness, and we must pray that He will anoint the doctor we are to see so that he makes the right diagnosis and prescribes the right treatment for us. We ourselves must keep our faith before we even take the medicine because our faith actually works with the medicine to make us whole. God intended it to be that way.

Dr. Marilyn Hughes Gaston, M.D., and Dr. Gayle K. Porter, Ph.D., shared the following in their book *Prime Time.* "Our words health and healing are from an Old English root word meaning 'whole.' And, of course, whole means . . . 'integration,' 'unity of all the parts; completeness.' So taking care of your mind, body, and spirit makes you whole and healthy." The Old English word "whole" is also the source of our word "holy." Our ancestors knew that healing and wholeness are holy, and, in fact, the work of the healers was considered to be a sacred task. The earliest physicians practiced their healing in temples and were thought to be holy men, women, or priests.

I feel the above statement pulls or ties together what has been said in this chapter and I'm happy that it is said by a physician and a psychiatrist, both Christians. It is great that some medical professionals are encouraging and supporting the practice of combining faith and medicine to transition to wholeness. We seek God first, to achieve holiness and wholeness.

Five

The Benefit of Faith in Medicine
for All Involved

Studies from universities and medical centers across the
country such as Duke, Johns Hopkins, Dartmouth, and San
Francisco General Hospital, have documented that the prevention of, and recovery from, emotional and physical illness, substance abuse, and surgery are significantly
influenced by our level of spiritual connectedness.

To draw on your spirituality and increase your
wellness, you need to assess and develop your conscious
practice of faith in daily life. You are a miracle and acting as
if we are miracles and developing a strong spiritual base
can both provide us with the moral courage we need to
make more difficult decisions and lifestyles changes. We
are all a part of a greater plan.

We all need to make ourselves first priority when it
comes to taking care of ourselves and others. I'm sure you
are wondering, "How am I taking care of others if I'm making myself first priority?" Well, if you don't take care of
yourself how can you help someone else? I make this statement in regards to patient, physician, caregiver, and liter-
ally everyone, ministers, too.

No one can be of service, providing care or treatment
to others, if they are weak, unequipped spiritually, and
malfunctioning. We have rendered ourselves null and

void, if you will, when we try to help others if we are in fact in need of help as well. It would be the blind leading the blind, trying to cross a major interstate, without benefit of a seeing eye dog. We need to be practical in all that we do. Remember, God says use wisdom.

We must be in good shape mentally, physically, and spiritually before we can be of help to anybody else. Making your healing a priority is going to mean focusing on your "wholeness" needs only, at the time of illness. Love yourself, nurture yourself, spend time with the Lord, relax, and concentrate on building up stronger and becoming your best ever!

Jesus said, "Love others as you love yourself." If you don't love yourself enough to take care of yourself, how can you take care of others, to show them that you love them? We can accomplish this with a little planning and adjusting our time, easy.

What I just suggested is not impossible and here are several suggestions to implement this practice:

1. Treat yourself to a special time "carved" into every day, just for you (it could be no more than thirty minutes).
2. Refresh your spirit by fueling your supply of God's word and the promises in His word.
3. Write notes of your thoughts or feelings and keep a record of special things and blessings, making a daily journal.

Encouraging or inspirational readings help to lift our spirit and soothe our mind and emotions. Physicians need this to help them face a day of sick people who will come to them for treatment. It will give them a sense of I'm not alone in this and God is my source of strength. It will keep them focused and ready to plan for the patient's health care. They need that added support for themselves from God and rely upon His guidance in all they do.

Patients need to build up their spirits to keep a positive mindset when the enemy strikes them with illness. They need to not allow fear to penetrate their thoughts and to not add concern to their family seeing the patient worried or afraid. The reading of encouraging and inspirational words will help them and the family, which are most likely going to be caregivers, in the event of surgery or any extended period of recovery from any illness.

Prayer is needed so the physician, patient, and family/caregivers all need to be actively praying to God. They all need to seek holy guidance and divine favor from the Lord. It is not just for the patient that they are to pray. They need to pray for themselves, and all those involved. They each make up the "treatment team," and they are intricate parts of the healing and recovery process.

God provided thousands of promises for his people and we should read those promises and trust Him at His word. Promises give us hope, and faith gives us trust for those promises to come to pass. Just reading God's promises makes us realize we can depend upon Him. Here are a few of the scriptures of His promises:

"Lord, your word is everlasting; it continues forever in heaven." (Psalm 119:89).
"The grass dies and the flowers fall, but the word of our God will live forever" (Isaiah 40:8).
"Praise the Lord! He promised He would give rest to His people, Israel, and He has given us rest. The Lord has kept all the good promises He gave through His servant Moses" (I Kings 8:56).

Even though the physician, patient, and family/caregivers are a "treatment team," they each must realize they are separate and therefore be acting responsibly on their own, for those things they must do in their respective roles. Our bodies are made up of many organs and cells, and they each perform whatever function they were designed to do. But they each depend on the other to maintain the body. The treatment team is of the same concept. Each should admit they need God in their life and role.

Dr. Henry Cloud, Ph.D., states in his book, *Changes that Heal,* "We need to realize our separateness. We need to develop time and interests separate from the time and interest of those we love." I agree with Dr. Cloud, we each have our own interests, responsibilities, and goals. I feel that we each need to develop our skills, increase our faith, pray, and maintain a relationship with God. By no means does this say that the treatment team should not pray corporately. It is very important that they feel a level of closeness, and they can come together for prayer, being that they are all believers in Christ (hopefully that is the case).

"God is strong and can help you not to fall and to present you before his glorious presence without fault and with great joy. He is the only God, the One who saves us. To Him be glory, majesty, power, and authority, through Jesus Christ our Lord, before all ages, past, now, and forevermore! Amen" (Jude 24–25). It is imperative that a patient keep the faith and fight a strong fight against the enemy. It is with confidence and faith during our illness that we come out the victor. Our minds and bodies are made strong by God's words in us and His hand upon us. "My child, pay attention to what I say. Don't ever forget my words; keep them always in your mind. They are the key to life for those who find them; they bring health to the whole body" (Proverbs 4:20–22).

Patients who are encouraged to use their faith and belief in God during illness experience fewer fears and concerns and have no uncertainty about the outcome of surgery or any disease they have. They learn to take each day in stride, with confidence and full assurance. Because they are calm and at ease, they realize that each day brings them more realization of wholeness again. The inner peace they experience allows them to rest and sleep, both of which they need for their bodies to heal effectively. "We know that in everything God works for the good of those who love Him. They are the people He called, because that was His plan. So what should we say about this? If God is with us, no one can defeat us" (Romans 8:28, 31).

Faith in God is our source of the strength He promised us:

"He gives me new strength. He leads me on paths that are right for the good of His name" (Psalm 23:3).
"God is our protection and our strength. He always helps in times of trouble" (Psalm 46:1).
"I am sad and tired. Make me strong again as you have promised" (Psalm 119:28).

The key to prosperity is seeking the Lord and prosperity is a word for all things, not just monetary or materially: "Beloved, I pray that you may prosper in all things and be in health, just as your soul prospers" (John 3:2).

In his book *You Are What You Think,* Dr. David Stoop states, "We create change in our lives by gaining control of our thoughts." Psalm 139:13–14 TLB says, "You made all the delicate, inner parts of my body, and knit them together in my mother's womb. Thank you for making me so wonderfully complex! It is amazing to think about. Your workmanship is marvelous." We must keep in mind that we are wonderfully made and that the same God that wonderfully made us can also wonderfully restore us. Faith in God and getting medical treatment is what is most needed when we are ill.

We have been taught that there is power in numbers and unity, and we have learned that it is true. When we come together on one accord and exercise our faith, positive things begin to happen. Jesus said, "Where two or three are gathered in my name, I am there also" (Matthew 18:20).

How powerful it is to have a team of believers uniting against the enemy. A spiritual army (treatment team) can conquer all things through Christ. Together the physician and patient can pray and seek God's instruction and guidance for the patient's health restoration. You already know the outcome is going to be awesome. They both benefit from having faith: the physician was anointed to treat the patient successfully, the patient's health was restored, and they both accomplished this through God.

According to Dr. Carol Svec, author of *After Any Diagnosis,* "the addition of psychologists and psychiatrists can be specifically helpful for people with illnesses. Therapists are often used to help patients control high blood pressure, reduce headache frequency, control chemotherapy side effects, change health-harming habits, and manage chronic pain. And some studies have shown that patients who receive counseling before surgery have shorter hospital stays, need less pain medicine, and have fewer complications."

The statistics given by Dr. Svec are very impressive, but just imagine how awesome the statistics would be if the therapist or counselor were Christian. That therapist would have the benefit of adding their faith with that of the patient and the faith-believing physician. Everyone on the team being of faith is an invaluable asset.

A faith-believing counselor would have the time and the opportunity to address or inquire about the patient's values, such as personal thoughts, feelings, and beliefs that the patient holds about health and life. The doctor cares about those things, but quite simply doesn't have the time to address them.

Susan Meltsner, M.S.W., author of *Body & Soul*, says that "Psychological fitness is part insight, part willingness to handle old situations in new ways, and a large measure of being backed up by other people, such as listeners, advisers, huggers (and butt kickers), friends."

Analyzing the statement of Susan Meltsner, a person of faith would have all the above with God, and the treatment team of faith. A mind that stays focused on the Lord, receives insight, knows that the Lord listens, advises, loves, and will chastise us, too. The team adds support in addition to all the love and support of God. Faith teams are an asset.

Nicholas Krommydas, Instructor in Pastoral Theology, Co-Director of Counseling and Spiritual Development at Hellenic College and Holy Cross School of Theology, stated the following: "Spiritual guidance in all cases is not just crisis intervention, but a continuous process, the movement to God and in God."

We are not to wait until we are in a situation of needing our health restored and a miracle, we need to be on a life-long pursuit of closeness and a deeper knowledge of the true and living God. We need to be striving to reach our divine destiny, as God has purposed for us. We need to be treated by a treatment team that is of like precious faith.

We need to attach ourselves to those who are of faith and seek services of Christians in the medical and psychological profession because you want to be connected in faith to those who operate by godly principles. We need to be having the people involved in our healing lifted up to and anointed by God.

The spiritual has always been a part of the healing process. There are scriptures that tell us of Jesus healing the sick through the spirit of God, the powers given Him by God. We also read of the physicians in the scriptures as well (i.e., Luke was Paul's personal physician). Paul had a physician of faith.

Richard R. Niebuhr, in his book, *Experiencing Religion*, states, "Many explain that modern man cannot believe in miracles; it is not that modern man cannot believe in miracles. It is just that he needs to be shown how."

The best way I feel to show that miracles do happen and how to receive a miracle is by showing those who are involved in your care and treatment who are not of faith. I have been in hospitals and seen by doctors who were called in by my primary physician (who is saved). I never hesitated to share my faith and the doctors got excited when they saw evidence of divine intervention on my behalf.

> "Is not personal conviction of faith a critical part of healing? The subject of healing and spirituality invites us to a critical, creative, difficult, and immensely important and fulfilling task. The question is not only one of integration, but also an invitation for spiritual renewal and reawakening, the concern of healing and spirituality is not only a call for holistic health labor, but also a challenge to produce the fruits of this labor . . . such as fellowships of healers, clinics, services to the needy, and missions."
> —John T. Chirban, editor of the book,
> *Medical, Psychological & Religious Dimensions*

The statement of John Chirban reinforces the fact that we should have the fellowship of those of like precious faith on our treatment team (healers, therapist, etc.) We must have the assurance of being in one accord and of knowing that all involved are receptive to the practice of welcoming in the Holy Spirit in the recovery and healing process.

Those on the treatment team can support each other and accomplish so much more because they are operating on faith (two or more, Jesus is there, also), they do not tire in their efforts because they cast their cares on the Lord. They do not get weary in their well-doing because their thoughts and strength will be renewed by the Lord.

Let those of like faith come and reason together, and seek wholeness one for another, from the Lord . . . our God!

Conclusion

In all that we do in life we can follow the lessons and examples given by Christ. Christ showed us how we are to live, share, love, and forgive others so that through all things we may be victorious. This covers our personal life, family, professional, and business issues as well. Christ was not just a healer, but He counseled those with other concerns as well (non-medical). He addressed all areas of the person's life, the physical health or body well-being, the spiritual, and the emotional (of the mind).

Jesus treated the entire being, the whole person. He knew that some of people's physical ills were caused by the emotions and psychology (mind), and had a direct relationship to their sins as well. When He healed, at times he simply said, "Thou sins are forgiven thee." He knew that the person's sin was accompanied by guilt, that depression was connected to the guilt, and the two manifest into physical symptoms of illness.

Whatever the profession a person has in life, whether it is a judge, teacher, scientist, designer, physician, counselor, etc., the Bible can be a guide, resource, valuable tool, or manual at hand.

God gave man a mind, a body and a spirit. He gave him all three for a reason. He put the three together because they each would enable man to function the way He intended and enable him to fulfill what he was called to do. When God has a plan, it will come to pass, and whatever

He creates has a purpose. How then should doctors not acknowledge the spirit of man when treating the body and mind of the patient?

People would heal faster and more completely, and get sick less often if doctors would treat holistically. We would see less cancer, less heart disease, fewer strokes, fewer nervous or emotional breakdowns, and fewer of all manner of conditions. Doctors who include faith, prayer, and counseling with some of their patients do see significant changes or benefits in the results of their treatment.

We would realize more long awaited and desired medical breakthroughs because God would be in the middle of it all. Treating a person's ills that may be emotional or spiritual in origin will be successful, in the true sense. Being whole means all parts are functioning in proper order and sound. How can man completely and effectively perform when part of him is out of connection with the rest of him? The answer, of course, is, not very well.

For people who suffer migraines caused by stress or tension caused by problems, taking aspirin or Tylenol would be like just drinking the water alone, without the pill. The help they need is of spiritual counseling. That would help them work through whatever issues are causing the stress. Tension would ease and the headache would cease.

Man will not be fully successful in obtaining excellent health care until the medical professional makes holistical medical treatment widespread. The full acceptance of God on the medical treatment team working with and through the medical staff and patient will ensure wholeness in the full sense. How can anything not be a success with God in charge and control? It is guaranteed to be awesome!

Man himself must take some responsibility for his own health and well-being by nurturing, feeding and

68

building up his whole being. He can start with a closer relationship with the Lord, more commitment to God, and definitely less committing of and more omission of sin. He needs to learn to follow the ways of Christ. People can not leave out growing in the knowledge of God, His holy scriptures, and learning the act of forgiving, and letting go of anger. We must learn to stop being people pleasers and begin pleasing the Lord our God.

When we seek to increase or grow more in faith, pray more, and keep God in the center of ALL things, we can be conquerors in all areas of our life. We need to push forward for the inclusion of God in the medical treatment field or profession. I mean push full steam ahead for the ultimate speed of its acceptance, worldwide. We need to get more Christian counselors included in treatment teams today because we need those trained in administering the word of God, using faith, prayer, and counseling to work on the behalf of those suffering from illness. We must attempt to open the doors of progress in an area new to some, but intended by God from the very beginning. There are patients who want the faith and spiritual addressed in their healing process, but are unsure of its availability and acceptability within the medical arena.

I did a "mini" survey just to test the waters, so to speak, in my local medical community about the acceptance or admission of the need to address faith and prayer when treating patients. I was amazed to find acceptance in a wide variety of medical specialties or practice areas. Below are the results of my survey:

Speciality or Field of Medicine	Highly Needed	Need	No Need
Urology	+		
Gynecology		+	
Internal Medicine	+		
Ear, Nose, Throat Specialist	+		
Physical Therapy	+		
Orthopedic Surgery	+		
General Surgery	+		
Dental Surgery	+		
Pulmonary/Respiratory		+	
Pharmacist	+		
Family Practice N.P.	+		
Radiologist	+		
Cardiology	+		
Family Practice M.D.	+		
Anesthesiologist	+		

The above survey results overwhelmed me and I got so excited! My heart was glad and I praised the Lord at each response. I have always desired to be a trail blazer for the Lord and this just made me want to get this area of acceptance pushed forward. But, of course, unless more minds of acceptance and doors are opened, the acknowledgment of the need in the area is of no use. We've got to get doors opened and minds renewed, or we can not go forward in getting God in the middle of medical treatment. I'm calling on prayer warriors of God to help pray down the walls of the barriers. I'm standing on faith . . . Amen!

Bibliography

Addictive Thinking and the Addictive Personality. Abraham J. Twerski, M.D. and Craig Nakken. MJF Books: New York, NY.

After Any Diagnosis. How to Take Action Against Your Illness Using the Best and Most Current Medical Information Available. Carol Svec. Three Rivers Press (Member of Crown Pub.): New York, NY.

Body and Soul: A Guide to Lasting Recovery from Compulsive Eating and Bulimia. Susan Meltsner, M.S.W. MJF Books: New York, NY (1993).

Changing Your Life with Changes that Heal. Dr. Henry Cloud. Ph.D. Zondervan Press.

The Faith Factor: Proof of the Healing Power of Prayer. Dale A. Mathews, M.D. with Connie Clark. Penguin Books: New York, NY (1998).

Handbook For Helping Others. Kenneth Stafford, Edited by Deborah D. Cole. Cornerstone Publishing, Inc. (Second Printing 1996).

Healing Mind, Healthy Woman: Using the Mind-Body Connection to Manage Stress and Take Control of Your Life. Alice D. Domar, Ph.D., and Henry Dreher.

The Healing Power of Prayer: The Surprising Connection between Prayer and Health. Chester L. Tolson, Ph.D. and Harold G. Koenig, M.D. Baker Books: Grand Rapids, MI.

The Healthy Life: How to Prevent and Reverse Today's Medical Threats. Cris C. Enriquez, M.D. Whitaker House.

Letting Go of Anger: The 10 Most Common Anger Styles and What to do About Them. Ron Potter-Efron M.S.W. and Pat Potter-Efron M.S. Barnes and Noble Books: New York, NY (1999).

Medical, Psychological and Religious Dimensions. John T. Chirban. University Press of America Lanham: New York, London.

Prayer: Understanding the Purpose and Power of Prayer, Earthly License to Heavenly Interference. Dr. Myles Munroe, Whitaker House.

Prime Time: The African American Women's Complete Guide to Midlife Health and Wellness. Marilyn Hughes-Gaston, M.D. Ballantine Publishing Group: New York, NY.

Self Nurture: Learning to Care for Yourself As Effectively As You Care for Everyone Else. Alice D. Domar, Ph.D. and Henry Dreher (2000).

7 Weeks to Emotional Healing. Joan Mathews Larson, Ph.D. Ballantine Wellspring trademark. Ballantine Publishing: New York, NY.

The Total De-Stress Plan: A Complete Guide to Working with Positive and Negative Stress. Beth MacEoin. Carlton Books Limited (2002).

You Are What You Think. David Stoop, Ph.D. Published by Fleming H. Revell, a division of Baker Books (1982, 1996, Third Print 2004).